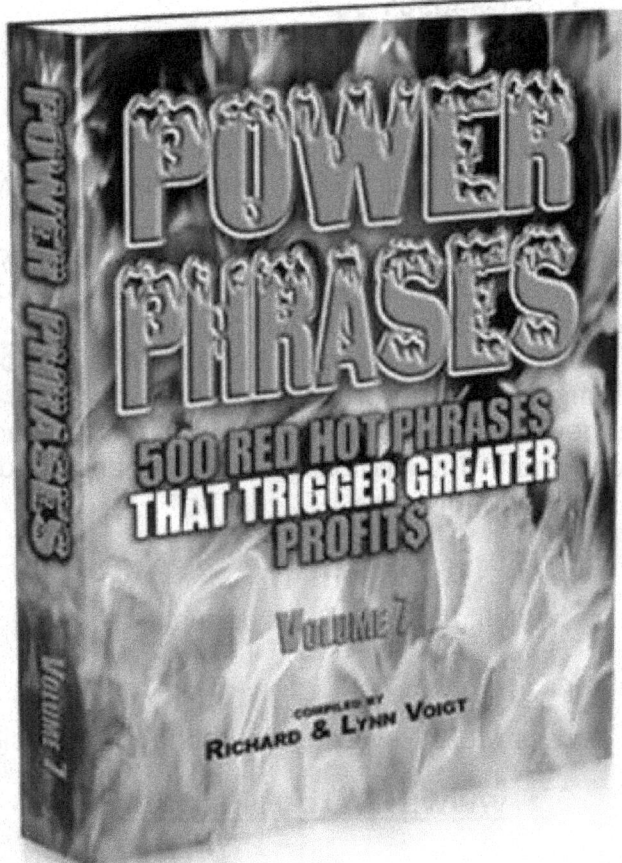

POWER PHRASES

500 RED HOT PHRASES THAT TRIGGER GREATER PROFITS

Volume 7

COMPILED BY
RICHARD & LYNN VOIGT

POWER PHRASES – Vol. 7
500 Power Phrases That Trigger Greater Profits

ISBN-13: 978-1-940961-06-4
ISBN-10: 1940961068

First Printing, 2013

Printed in the United States of America

To Access More Powerful Marketing Tools Visit:

www.RIVObooks.com

www.RIVOinc.com

www.WisconsinGarden.com

POWER

PHRASES

Volume 7

500 POWER PHRASES THAT TRIGGER GREATER PROFITS

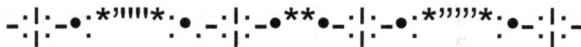

-·|·--•·*’”"""*·•·_·|·_•*|·_•**•_·|·_•·*’””*·•·_|·-
·•|·•·   ·•·_·|·_•·|·-   ·|·-

Compiled by

Richard & Lynn Voigt
I.M. Education Specialists

Introduction:

Powerful Phrases, Headlines, Sub Headlines, Slogans, Bullet Points and Interview Sound Bites are perhaps the most powerful marketing tools mankind has ever created. They are the lifeblood behind every business venture are the ultimate secret weapon of Millionaire Marketers.

No matter whether you are introducing or promoting a brand new product, teaching a "How To" skill, building a website, or simply sending an email, using the perfect power phrase is crucial to capturing and holding eyeballs and producing greater marketing profits.

In today's world every word you use has measurable impact. Each word can produce emotional psychological buttons that trigger psychological reactions. Successful advertisers understand that using an effective power phrase is a true art form that turns "wants" into instant gratification "needs." Once artfully triggered, any niche market can instantly create more protifable conversions.

Now it's your turn to personalize this incredible collection of 500 Power Phrases in ways that instantly advance your own effective marketing skills as you create new and power phrases, slogans, presentations, bullet points, or interview sound bites that take you to the next level.

Whether starting or running a small business, writing an ad, coming up with a memorable slogan, making a major corporate presentation, bullet points, creating a video, writing a book, searching for the perfect slogan, teaching a lesson or book report, your creative use of these Power Phrases can capture more eyeballs and produce some amazing rewards quickly turning you into a Marketing Genius. Now, it's your turn to make the magic happen!

POWER PHRASES

Volume 7 – 3001 - 3500

500 Power Phrases That Trigger Greater Profits

Begin Selecting & Customizing Your Perfect Marketing Phrase

3001	7 Reasons Why You Must Start Your Own Business TODAY
3002	Best of The Michel Fortin Blog in 2008
3003	Stealing Ideas From Nature
3004	Weather Is A Mood, Climate Is A Personality
3005	Create Your Own Products
3006	The Art Of Marketing Mind Control
3007	Embrace The Contrast
3008	Fair Warning - We May Remove It At Any Time
3009	They're Just Trying To Get Your Attention
3010	How To Automate Your Online Business
3011	Getting An Emotional Fix
3012	How To Get And Register A Google Email Account
3013	Expand Your Bank Vault With This Bottom Line Approach
3014	You Can Never Have Enough Sub Headlines
3015	How To Fail Giving Away Free Money
3016	Develop Your Profit Instincts
3017	Provide It Different Ways
3018	When You Go Paperless
3019	Free Shocking Video
3020	Wanna Work For Me
3021	How Do You DO IT With Words

3022	Automated Business Builder
3023	New Summer Scandals
3024	We Only Act In The NOW
3025	Desire Leads To Action
3026	Must Have Certain Set Of Skills
3027	Act Now To Learn More
3028	What Are You Working On
3029	Qualities Tougher To Quantify
3030	Create The Highest Caliber B3B Cast Ever Assembled
3031	Adding To The Economic Pie
3032	Earn Extra Marketing Credit Points
3033	In Only 30 Minutes
3034	Customers Proven To Buy
3035	Commission Thieves Are A Very Real Threat
3036	The Work Is Well Worth It
3037	Suspicious Activity Reports
3038	We Got Sick Of The Daily Grind
3039	Take Your Time But Hurry
3040	Your I.M. Retirement Plan
3041	The Brain Is Built To Respond
3042	Mini-Course With An Attention Grabbing Name
3043	Are Mp3s Illegal
3044	Informative And Straight To The Point
3045	Enable And Inspire
3046	Communicate And Lead Through Powerful Stories
3047	Exactly Who Are You Trying To Reach
3048	Zig Zagging Doesn't Lead To Happiness
3049	Think Long Term
3050	When Times Are Good
3051	What Does A Millionaire Look Like
3052	Real World Traffic
3053	The Moment Of My Big Breakthrough
3054	A Revolutionary Program Providing Unlimited Possibilities
3055	Prove The Naysayer Dead Wrong
3056	Let's Get Moving
3057	Failure Is Not Forever
3058	Engage Them Within 3 Seconds
3059	Execution Strategies That Produce Huge Profits

3060	When You're Grown Up
3061	Automate Your Payday
3062	It's About The Life You Want
3063	Your Video Showcase
3064	Free Trial Offer
3065	Hot Weekly Deals
3066	Cold Hard Truths
3067	The Safelist Directory Ebook
3068	Hardcore Proof From An Affiliate Master
3069	Generate All The Referrals You'll Ever Need
3070	Win Money Online
3071	Maven Of Your Market Niche
3072	Savvy Street Smart Lessons
3073	Fundamental Actions You Need To Take Right Now
3074	The Highest Impact Categories
3075	Take A Vacation Whenever You Want
3076	Ready For Whirlwind Exposure
3077	High Quality
3078	Does Your Bosshole Act Like He's Doing You A Favor
3079	Think Extensively Not Intensively
3080	Start Stacking Your Dollars
3081	Maintaining A High Variety Of Content
3082	Advertise Just About Any Product Or Service
3083	Your Opportunity To Set The Price
3084	Quick Cash Certificates
3085	Blast Those Roadblocks Away
3086	How Did They Find This
3087	Just For Your
3088	Get Star Treatment
3089	Is Your Site Under-Performing
3090	Changing Friends Faster Than Underwear
3091	Advertiser Offers Humongous FREE Ad Space
3092	What Is It That You Do Exactly
3093	Incredible Energetic And Positive Responses
3094	No Time No Energy
3095	Prying Identity Theft
3096	It's Vitally Important
3097	Research For Effective Article Writing

3098	We Are Here To Push You Forward
3099	What Do You Do Just For Fun
3100	Get The Right Ideas In Your Head
3101	For All Your Girlfriends
3102	When Value Is Clear Decisions Are Easy
3103	Arresting Sales Slumps
3104	Follow Up On A Regular Basis
3105	Scare Yourself Into Bettering Yourself Fast
3106	All Aren't Dogs Equal Woof Woof
3107	Practices That Threaten Survival
3108	Tweak And Refine
3109	Face Your Fears
3110	My Push Button Empire Wants You
3111	Joint Venture Investor
3112	Go Ahead Drop Your Blog On Me
3113	Viable Balance
3114	Free Landing Page
3115	You'll Find This Is Actually More Than A Little Misleading
3116	Adopting Creative Thinking
3117	Too Busy Doing It Wrong
3118	Why We Want You To Be Rich
3119	Are You Wasting Your Time Creating False Value
3120	Do The Right Thing Online And Reap Incredible Rewards
3121	But Wait There's More
3122	Success And Family Aren't Incompatible
3123	Industry Leading 100% Money Back Guarantee
3124	They Have No Clue Who's Behind It
3125	Changing Consumer Habits
3126	My Hard-Earned Secrets
3127	Be In Control Of Your Own Destiny
3128	Now Being Allocated
3129	Where Your Prospects Are
3130	On The Road To Success
3131	Want To Wiggle More Orders Your Way
3132	Start Banking Profits Immediately
3133	Discover The Coolness Inside
3134	Become Conscious Of Facial Expressions
3135	Need An Estimate

3136	There Really Is No Downside
3137	Need An Occasional Kick In The Butt
3138	Create An Order-Pulling Niche
3139	Gallons Of Sweat
3140	Pamper Your Marketing Problem Away
3141	Before Your Feet Hit The Ground
3142	9 Out Of 10 People Have Never Read An eBook
3143	A Better Way To Steal Traffic
3144	Still Listening To What Others Think You Can't Do
3145	Make Your Computer Impenetrable
3146	Here's Your Shiny New Password
3147	Direct From The Marketing World
3148	Worth Your While Looking
3149	Do You Still Have Something To Prove
3150	The Truth vs. The Real Truth
3151	Why Multilingual Sites Make More Money
3152	Like An Easter Egg Hunt
3153	Affiliate Commerce Frenzy
3154	Unlimited Number Of Ideas
3155	This Is How It Works
3156	How Much Should I Charge For This Content
3157	Work Directly With Out-Sourced Workers
3158	Piggyback On Free Traffic
3159	You'll Want To Do This Today
3160	Special Period Of Excellent Opportunity
3161	We Too Take Part
3162	Stop Being An Entrepreneur
3163	Reap The Real Rewards Online
3164	You Need To Read This Page Now Because…
3165	Find Your Alone Time
3166	Focusing On Results
3167	Penalty Flags To Watch For
3168	Does This Piece Resonant
3169	For Under Performing Products
3170	Subscribers Are Racking Up Big Time Commission Checks
3171	Calling All Property Owners
3172	Some Think I Must Be Crazy
3173	Essential Autoresponder Tips

3174	I'm Gonna Take Advantage Of Your Temporary Insanity
3175	Enter The Headline Spectacularity Zone
3176	Marketing Receiver
3177	Reinforce Beneficial Solutions
3178	Thou Shall Find More With Less
3179	Ready To Buy
3180	My Life Had Purpose Again
3181	Business Goldmine
3182	Offline Consulting Step By Step
3183	Win The Jackpot
3184	That Someone Can Be You
3185	I Just Can't Tell Everyone
3186	A Free Ticket To My Telecast
3187	Create Your Own Personal Ad System
3188	Just Be You
3189	Driven By Irrational Passion
3190	Online Presentation LIVE Tomorrow
3191	And I Thought They Wanted My Business
3192	Only $7 To Start A Business - Yes
3193	Money-Back-Plus Guarantee
3194	Powerful Self-Help Program
3195	This Tactic Could Make Or Break You
3196	Pick Your Plan Now
3197	Find Out Who's Talking
3198	The Monthly Pay Model
3199	I Just Love Giving Money Away
3200	Scale Plus Automation
3201	How To Create Your Own Lead Pulling Squeeze Page
3202	Distract Yourself
3203	How Well Do You Manage Risk
3204	Transferable Master Resale Rights
3205	Video Streaming
3206	Redesign Your Life
3207	Those With A Plan Or Those With Money
3208	Our Lives Are Entangled
3209	Does Your Business Overlook This Glaring Hole
3210	Incredible Graphic Designs
3211	I'm Living Proof This System Works

3212	Turn Up Your Speakers And Watch This Video Right Now
3213	How To Find A Properly Focused Action Plan
3214	Last Seat Being Jerked Out Under You
3215	Start Off With A Couple Of Short Stories
3216	Most Frustrating Part About Starting An Online Business
3217	True Or False You Have No Worries
3218	My Advice - Go There Now
3219	One Great Price
3220	Cantankerous Customers
3221	Keep It Under 3 Minutes
3222	This Requires Imagination
3223	Organize Life On Your Terms
3224	Make More Money Invisibly
3225	The Most Valuable Asset On Earth
3226	Master Abilities That Can't Be Outsourced
3227	Using Bold Print Or Underlines
3228	We'll Bill You Later
3229	How To Turn Your Business Around Virtually Overnight
3230	Milking Monday Meetings
3231	Why Our Members Learn More While Making More Money
3232	What's A One Percenter
3233	Free Video Blog Series
3234	Why Drip Feeding Is More Effective
3235	Proven Spectacularly Profitable
3236	Here's What You'll Discover Before Anyone Else
3237	No Cheesy One Time Deals Here
3238	It's Not What You Do - It's How You Do It
3239	Inventing New Reasons For Failure
3240	Track Links To External Sites And Services
3241	No Experience Necessary
3242	Want To Listen Without Reading The PDF
3243	Long Hours And Still Nothing To Show
3244	No Longer Just Part Of The Herd
3245	This Manual Provides A Fresh Start
3246	Too Many Jokers Online
3247	Today's Gonna Be Fun
3248	Focus On Building Great Opt-In Lists
3249	Social Search Is Shifting

12

3250	It Isn't Only Luck Anymore
3251	Even In Darker Times
3252	Don't Let My Insanity Turn You On
3253	Live Your Message
3254	How To Implement The Perfect Backend Strategy
3255	Get In Front Of The Camera Everyday
3256	Get Incredible FREE Research About Hot Offers... Right Now!
3257	The Secret To Unleashing Your Genius
3258	How These Cannibalize Sales
3259	Hold A Free Teleseminar
3260	Marketing Incursions
3261	What Are You Missing
3262	When Diseases Weren't Yet Invented
3263	Earn A Deeper Level Of Trust
3264	Refer People To Membership Sites
3265	Delve Deep Into This Niche
3266	The Most Important Technique Ever Known To Mankind
3267	Give Them Less Incentive To Steal
3268	The Format Is Simple
3269	New 60 Page Guide
3270	There Will Be More Pain
3271	One On One
3272	You Don't Even Need A Website
3273	From The Vault
3274	America's Foremost Millionaire
3275	Beyond Keywords
3276	Check This Box For Your Bonus
3277	This Book Is Really That Powerful
3278	It Just Got A Whole Lot Better
3279	Stop Begging
3280	Secrets You'll Never Learn From Anyone Else
3281	Trouble Converting
3282	If You Only Do It Once
3283	Looking For A Lucrative Compensation Plan
3284	Stop Them From Stealing Your Products
3285	Blast Your Site To Uncharted Heights
3286	You're Not Coming Down Slowly
3287	Who, What, When, Where, and Why

3288	Purchases Start With Trust
3289	I'll Cut Out The Suspense
3290	On A Rampage Of Appreciation
3291	Questionable Damage
3292	Don't Play Marketing Games With Customers
3293	Sunny Sunday Saver
3294	Cycle Through Everything You Know
3295	Don't Miss This Wonderful Opportunity
3296	We Have Some Presents For You
3297	Free Upon Request
3298	Stay Grounded Into Your Body
3299	Ditch The Quilt
3300	A Video Without A Video Camera Or Microphone
3301	Raising Your Energy Levels
3302	Pick Up A Marketing Hobby
3303	Put Audio Ads On Your Website
3304	Sharing Similar Frames Of Reference
3305	New Products Pop Up Each Day
3306	Let Me Be Brutally Blunt
3307	Your Service Provider Doesn't Know Jack
3308	The Breathing Space You Need
3309	The More Specific The Better
3310	Can't Afford It
3311	Duplication Of Successful Marketing Efforts
3312	Maybe This Is Suppose To Happen
3313	What Happens At The End Of The Day
3314	Profit Guide Full Of Tips Tricks And Tactics
3315	More Sales For The Same Effort
3316	Are They Biting On You Niche
3317	Out Of Ideas
3318	The Different Parameters Of Success
3319	Find Your Comfort Zone
3320	How Can You Possibly Go Back The Old Way
3321	Every Imaginable Niche Has A Market
3322	I Found You A New Job
3323	After 9 Months It's Finally Born
3324	It's Hard To Walk And Chew Gum
3325	Dogs Need A Knowledgeable Trainer And So Do People

14

3326	All Work Is Run By Technology
3327	Winners Emerge
3328	Move Forward With Confidence
3329	Knowing Where You've Been
3330	Your Brand Disappearing Without A Trace
3331	Finally Someone Is Blasting These Wannabe Scams
3332	Pay $7 One Time
3333	Marketing Disaster Has Created Huge Opportunities
3334	Stop Fretting Over Pennies
3335	Predictable Scalable And Consistent
3336	Is This Your Missing Link
3337	Direct Result Of Tiny Simple Changes
3338	Before You Open Up
3339	Do You Use It
3340	Afraid To Answer The Phone
3341	Who Is The Decision Maker
3342	Turn Your Points Into Cash Money
3343	Got A Phone Pencil And Pad Of Paper
3344	People Will Eventually Get It
3345	At A Price Anyone Can Afford
3346	An Accomplished Liar
3347	Action Required
3348	Best Freebie In The World
3349	Normal Means Mediocre
3350	Speak With Passion
3351	Entering Negative Territory
3352	I Get It Now
3353	Why Work So Hard For Something You'll Never Own
3354	Cash Back Without Thinking
3355	Sure Fire Profit Plans
3356	The Hub Of Creative Thoughts
3357	All About Giving Value
3358	The Actions That Create The Money
3359	The Next Step Was
3360	My Bottom Line
3361	A Few Hours Per Week Of Your Time
3362	Commit To Your Vision
3363	World's Greatest Response

3364	The Secret Is Out
3365	Want To Fill Your Piggy Bank
3366	They're All Free Once You Come Inside
3367	Offer Yourself The Gift Of Success
3368	You Have To Know How This Feels
3369	Your Best Weapon For Success
3370	I Don't Mind
3371	Hosting Secrets Revealed
3372	Simplicity Rules In Copy Writing
3373	Get A Good Night's Sleep
3374	Deathwatch Of The Gold Watch And 40-Year Pension
3375	I'll Be Quick
3376	Fall Into Wisconsin
3377	Has Theirs Ever Made You Money
3378	2 Second Page Loads
3379	Flow Of Energy Flows To Action
3380	Freeze Your Money By Not Wasting It On These Mistakes
3381	Avoid Fashion Logos On Videos
3382	A Crisis Can Erupt At Any Moment
3383	Will eReaders Become A Necessity
3384	Instantly Profit From Subscribers
3385	Quit Being A Lab Rat
3386	Overlooking Simple Solutions
3387	Minnows vs. Whales Marketing
3388	Two Possible Fates
3389	Do You Have An Ask Campaign
3390	Simple & Practical
3391	Find 10 Emotional Niches
3392	Understanding Client's Wants And Needs
3393	One Succinct Paragraph
3394	Becoming Your Message
3395	Original Profound And Amazingly Thought Provoking
3396	It's Never One Size Fits All In This Market
3397	Are You Ready To Roar
3398	Need Answers Fast
3399	You'll Get Everything You Need To Customize This
3400	The Big Lie
3401	Jump In While The Water Is Still Warm

16

3402	Become Transparent And Real
3403	It's Not Easy At First
3404	Future Weapons
3405	For Those Who Don't Like To Read
3406	What You Believe Can Limit Your Success
3407	It's LIVE Go Go Go
3408	Your Life's Dreams Lie Just Ahead
3409	Internet Marketing Can Be Hard
3410	You Know What They Want
3411	Eyes Are The Mirrors To Your Soul
3412	Zero Risk Looking And Listening
3413	Being Secure Has Nothing To Do With Your Job
3414	Dust It Off
3415	See What I Just Developed
3416	Take Control Of Your Customers
3417	An Emotional Connection With Another Human Being
3418	Bottom Up Preference
3419	They Will Pay You With Their Time
3420	Do Your Header Graphics Suck
3421	How Self-Deceit Ultimately Destroys Success
3422	Seize The Moment
3423	Only $10 More And You Get Them Both
3424	At Absolutely No Cost To You
3425	The Best Damn Dollar I Ever Spent
3426	Timely Action Is Required Now
3427	Keep A Consistent Conversational Tone
3428	Looking Forward To The New One
3429	Why Successful Businesses Focus On What's In It For Them
3430	Need High Quality Resources
3431	Monetization Tip To Make High Commissions
3432	Build The Muscle Skill And Habit
3433	Internet Money-Maker Madness Is Here
3434	Flood Your PP Account With Payments
3435	Eliminate All The Guess Work
3436	Start Leading The Way
3437	Just The Facts
3438	Sick And Tired Of The Drudgery
3439	Please Check Your Email For The Information You Requested

17

3440	Edit Two Files
3441	Who Else Wants To Earn Money & Respect
3442	Click Here To Apply
3443	No Advertising Budget - No Problem
3444	Take A Look At These Screen Shots
3445	Don't Take Retirement Sitting Down
3446	Turn On Even The Most Disinterested Prospects
3447	Becoming A Seasoned Pro Without The Missteps
3448	You Have To Be Strong
3449	A Confused Mind Never Buys
3450	You Already Have A Specialty
3451	Sunggle Under Your Technology Blanket
3452	Don't Let Them Pull The Wool Over Your Eyes
3453	The Perfect Combination
3454	On Fire With New Bonuses
3455	Writing A Book Will Change Your Life
3456	Don't Become A Slave To Your Computer
3457	But You Already Knew That
3458	Create Good Backgrounds
3459	Give People Options
3460	Still Jumping Through Marketing Hoops
3461	Is This Too Good To Be True
3462	Connection And Inspiration
3463	How To Upsell With Extended Benefits
3464	Thousands Have This Priceless Gift But Never Discover It
3465	A Job Is Only 2 Paychecks From Disaster
3466	The Barrier To Feeling Successful
3467	My Gamble Finally Paid Off
3468	Task Bar Raises Glass To Success
3469	Push The Boundaries To Explore Its Profit
3470	There's Nothing Wrong With Wanting More
3471	Life Requires Asking
3472	Blogospheres Have Evolved Into Money-Making Machines
3473	Clean The Stupid Out Of Their Ears And Listen Up
3474	Before They Lost Their Way
3475	These Will Sell Out Fast
3476	Feed Yourself Figuratively
3477	Are You Hearing I Want What You Have

3478	Listen Up
3479	How To Have What You Want
3480	Digging Down Deep
3481	We're Not That Different
3482	Generate Keyword Lists
3483	Only 10 Percent Of The Additional Revenue Brought In
3484	Take Happiness Seriously
3485	Do You Know Who's Following You
3486	I Re-Doubled My Efforts
3487	Hit Record And Start Talking
3488	This Is Who I Am
3489	Giving Yourself A Raise Without Asking Your Boss
3490	You Can Enroll Now
3491	Take Just One Piece And Experience Success
3492	Okay Where Is The Catch
3493	Blue Prints For Success Are Always Built Upon A System
3494	Overcome Obstacles
3495	Occupied My Thoughts Every Hour Of The Day
3496	Work At Your Leisure
3497	Easiest Way To Customize Your Own Site
3498	A Serendipitous Way To Start
3499	Five In One Products
3500	Self-Stamped Envelope That Brings Results

Lynn and I hope that this "Think Tank" volume series of 500 Hot Phrases will helped you clearly paint your dreams, sell your ideas, and market your messages, propelling each of your ideas and projects toward incredible success. Watch for our next Volume!

We truly wish you the very best and look forward to hearing your success stories.

Concluding Thoughts:

Ever success is built upon a preparing a strong foundation, having a clear vision, and taking positive action each and every day. If you've been searching for a new lifestyle, then you'll find this book directive and inspirational. You can open it to any page and let that page help you rethink possibilities, consider new ideas, open new opportunities, and ultimately experience a more successful and fulfilling lifestyle.

Every problem has a solution! Regardless of your current situation or circumstance, know that you have the power and responsibility to redirect your life in any direction you choose. Simply start thinking about and research the kind of lifestyle that truly appeals to your heart. Begin your new journey by learning everything you can about your chosen subject. When you make that commitment, you'll open more unexpected doors to unique opportunities than imagined.

**"Creative Thought Is The Only Reality
Everything Else Is Merely The By-Product Of That Thought."**
- Walter Russell

So why not start thinking **BIGGER? It won't cost you any more.** It all starts by never allowing your current life's situation, environment, or so-called friends to limit your path to a happier, healthier, and successful life. After all, whose life is this?

Make a decision to focus on learning something new each and every day. Begin attracting your ideal lifestyle by doing something you love and enjoy. As difficult as it may be, don't allow money to limit your dreams. Focus on the kind of thoughts that make you feel good. Once you learn how to control your focus, you'll have a great chance to see your dreams take shape. You've finally learn to harness the power you always had within, a Universal Energy stream that flows 365/24/7 in any direction your project your thoughts, Good or Bad. Want proof? The thoughts you currently believe and project reflect the life you're currently living. Therefore, if your life isn't happening, change your thoughts, and change your life. It's something only you can hold, visualize, and project, living your dream come true.

Find yourself a mentor and spend more time with people who truly appreciate, support, and foster your dreams. Life may be short, but the thoughts we hold can make our life wider and more fulfilling.

20

About The Authors:

Richard and Lynn develop creative strategies that paint dreams, sell ideas, & market messages   Together, they present a unique team-approach, working side-by-side, helping clients pursue their passions while sharing their skills and diverse expertise as authors, artists, inventors, entrepreneurs, & Internet marketing education specialists.

Teaching by example, they mentor proven self-publishing services, graphic design, video production, domain acquisition, and marketing research of behalf of their company, RIVO Inc – RIVO Marketing, since 1997. They've created & produced hundreds of videos, self-published dozens of books on a wide variety of topics and created thousands of original works of fine art, while refining their Internet Marketing techniques, mentoring programs, and related business website development.

Their mission is to continually uncover new products and services, test new strategies, and network useful solutions with off and online entrepreneurs, small business owners, writers, local artists, models, teachers, students, and marketing professionals.

Their goal is to help clients create an action plan that discovers and connects the missing pieces of the success puzzle. The goals they foster create multiple streams of income for today's volatile economic climate. Their motto is: "Do the work once and allow the work to create additional streams of income for a lifetime."

Feel free to contact them if you have questions or would like to tap into their talents and expertise. They appreciate your feedback and look forward to hearing your success stories.

Contact:
Richard & Lynn Voigt - RIVO
I. M. Education Specialists

RIVO INC - RIVO Marketing
13720 West Keefe Avenue
Brookfield, Wisconsin 53005 – USA
Email: support@RIVOinc.com
Website: www.RIVObooks.com
Website: www.WisconsinGarden.com

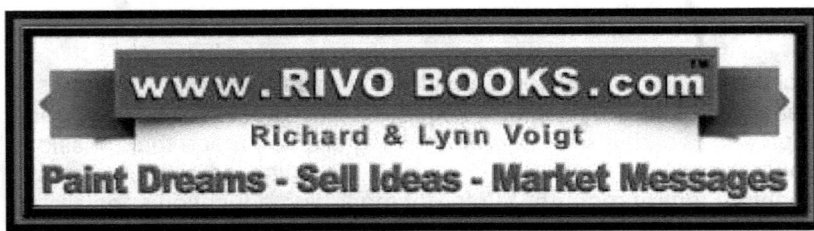

Visit Lynn's Garden: www.WisconsinGarden.com
view hundreds of great garden video blogs Tips

See Richard's Unique Artwork: www.RIVOart.com
view over 3,000 original Fine-Art compositions

Our Book Titles Now Available On Amazon:

THE GOLDEN VAULT OF MOTIVATIONAL QUOTATIONS
Words of Wisdom from The Greatest Minds & Leaders

BABY NAME .ME - 21,400 Names & Nicknames
For Family, Friends, Pets, Natural & Man-Objects

DOODLE DESIGNS Volumes 1-3
For Professionals & Kids Of All Ages
DOODLE DESIGNS – Vol. 1
DOODLE DESIGNS – Vol. 2
DOODLE DESIGNS Coloring Book Vol. 3

Work MORE Accomplish LESS Get FIRED!

ACTION HEADLINES That Drive Emotions – Volumes 1- 6
 Paint Dreams, Sell Ideas & Market Your Message
Action Headlines That Drive Emotions Vol. 1
Action Headlines That Drive Emotions Vol. 2
Action Headlines That Drive Emotions Vol. 3
Action Headlines That Drive Emotions Vol. 4
Action Headlines That Drive Emotions Vol. 5
Action Headlines That Drive Emotions Vol. 6

IDIOMS – IDIOMS - IDIOMS
6,450 Popular Expressions That Put Words In Your Mouth

The CLICHÉ BIBLE - 8,400 Clichés For Sports Fanatics
& Lovers Of Popular Expressions

MORE THAN WORDS
5000+ Marketing Phrases That Sell

HYPNOTIC PHRASING
WARNING-This Book Teaches You How To Grab Eyeballs

YOUR RIGHT TO WEALTH
Becoming Wealthy Isn't Hard When You Know How

WI GARDEN – Let's Get Dirty
Our Wisconsin Garden Guide Promoting Delicious, Healthier Home-Grown
Fresh Food, With Tools, Tips, & Ideas That Inspire Gardeners!

MONETIZE YOUR SOCIAL LIFE
Earn Extra Income While Having Fun Online

BABY NAMES
21,400 Unique Baby Names & Nicknames

FUNNY HEADLINES vol. 1
3,500 Outrageous Silly Brain Toots

FUNNY HEADLINES vol. 2
3,500 Outrageous Silly Brain Toots

JOBS
10,240 Career Paths That Can Change Your Life!

MONEY WORDS
Powerful Phrases That Million Dollar Copywriters Use To Make Piles Of
Cash On Demand!

GARDEN QUOTATIONS
400 Garden Quotes From The Earth To Your Soul

HEADLINE STARTERS
175,000 Words That Paint Dreams, Sell Ideas, And Market Your Message

BABY NAMES
25,350 Baby Names & Nicknames For Your Family Friends & Pets
    697 pages 7,000 Names with Origin & Meaning plus Top 100 Names,
    And 2,000 Most Popular Names

CURIOUS WORDS
15,800 Words That Expand Your Mind And Change Your Life

INSPIRING THOUGHTS
That Inspire Happiness, Success & A Clearer Understanding Of Life

MARKETING EYEBALLS
100 Ideas That Can Add Unlimited Subscribers To Your Lists

SECOND OF FIVE
My Early Years- From Birth To High School

POWER PHRASES – Individual Volumes 1 - 10
500 Power Phrases That Trigger Greater Profits

POWER PHRASES Pro Edition – Volumes 1-10 (Complete Series)
5000 Power Phrases That Trigger Greater Profits

COMING SOON! – BE THE FIRST TO GRAB YOUR PRO COPY

POWER PHRASES Pro Edition Volumes 1-10 (Complete Series)
5000 Power Phrases That Trigger Greater Profits

What do Marketing Millionaires know that you don't? They know how to pull money out of thin air by using their secret language of Power Phrases.

This Pro Edition of 5000 Red Hot Power Phrases not only saves you time and money but will help jump-start your creative brain in ways you may have never considered. Simply open this amazing collection to any page and find your perfect power phrase. All it may take is simply adding or replacing ONE word. It's simple, quick, and easy!

1. **Want to create more powerful profitable campaign offers?**
2. **Thinking of revitalizing a more professional business identity?**
3. **Want to update old product or service media advertisements?**
4. **Searching for fresh ideas that could improve sales and profits?**
5. **Looking for brand new ways to create stronger media sales copy?**
6. **Ready to use millionaire strategies advancing you to the next level?**

5000 POWER PHRASES is exclusively for professional Internet Marketers, authors,advertisers, executives, business owners, TV & radio reporters, entrepreneurs, administrators, managers, supervisors, teachers and students who want to find and access unique phrases for marketing slogans, presentation bullet points, and interview sound bites that powerfully paint dreams, sell ideas, and market your message.

Stop wasting valuable time, money, and energy racking your brain for new ideas. Create more profitable power phrase marketing campaigns for all your products, services, slogans, bullet points, and interview sound bites that finally grab and hold people's attention and trigger greater profits?

You now have a very powerful and professional marketing tool in your hand. We are confident that you know how to use it wisely in order to maximize the potential of all your marketing campaigns! Lynn and I **Thank You** for your support and purchase.

CLAIM 500 MORE POWER PHRASES!

Thank you for purchasing this eBook and in doing so we would like to send you **500 More Red Hot Power Phrases for FREE!**

When you post a **positive review of this Book on Amazon Books** under this title you'll receive an additional **500 POWER PHRASES.** Your review may also be sent directly to us.

Your request must be received within 30-days of purchase. Once your positive Book review is posted and verified, simply email the following to **(500@RIVOinc.com)**:

1. Full Name of Purchaser
2. Email address
3. Paypal Invoice Number
4. Copy of your posted Book Review*

Once we receive the above, we'll send you 500 Power Phrases **(PDF)** emailed to the address you provided.

Visit: www.RIVObooks.com for additional volumes as they become available including the Pro Edition of 5000 Red Hot Power Phrases that say what you mean to say and trigger greater profits.

Lynn and I look forward to your written comments and suggestions as we love hearing from each of our readers.

Richard & Lynn Voigt
RIVO Inc – RIVO Marketing
13720 West Keefe Avenue
Brookfield, Wisconsin 53005 USA
Telephone: (262) 783-5335
www.RIVObooks.com

P. S. If you love gardening, catch us on www.WisconsinGarden.com

*NOTE: This offer is valid providing it does not violate the terms of service of the entity with whom you made this purchase. Duplicate or incomplete entries will also not be eligible and this offer is limited to one request per email address. All eligible review submissions become the property of RIVO Inc - RIVO Marketing – RIVO books and may be used as promotional testimonials ads on RIVO Inc websites. This offer may be withdrawn at any time without prior written notice.